THE SUGAR MILE

By Glyn Maxwell

POETRY

Tale of the Mayor's Son

Out of the Rain

Rest for the Wicked

The Breakage

The Boys at Twilight: Poems 1990–1995

Time's Fool: A Tale in Verse

The Nerve

The Sugar Mile

PLAYS

Wolfpit

Broken Journey

The Last Valentine

Anyroad

The Only Girl in the World

The Lifeblood

Best Man Speech

THE SUGAR MILE

Glyn Maxwell

HOUGHTON MIFFLIN COMPANY

BOSTON NEW YORK 2005

For information about permission to reproduce selections
from this book, write to Permissions, Houghton Mifflin Company,
215 Park Avenue South, New York, New York 10003.

Visit our Web site: www.houghtonmifflinbooks.com.

Library of Congress Cataloging-in-Publication Data
Maxwell, Glyn, 1962–
The sugar mile / Glyn Maxwell.
p. cm.
ISBN 0-618-56243-5
I. Title.
PR6063.A869S84 2005
811'.54—dc22 2004060936

Printed in the United States of America

Book design by Lisa Diercks
The text of this book is set in Dante.

QUM 10 9 8 7 6 5 4 3 2 1

I

SEPTEMBER 8TH, BROADWAY & 86TH

I wrote at the top of breath
not having reached it. At the top of breath

the skyline is a shoreline
seen from high above. Buildings are sand

and peter out. All land
is a ledge, all space is a drop, all steps have a nerve.

There can be no first person.
I fill my lungs to go and the first person's

yards ahead. Then he jumps.
Then I look and he falls and falls until my lungs

are veal and I'm alone.
I write *I* and it leaks like a first inkpen.

The poet is any stranger
seen today, whose past is an empty moleskine

tugged from a pocket, laid
sealed on the bar like this one is. He shifts

and it's evening in a mirror,
peek-a-boo through a platoon of optics

as he begins, resembling
any stranger, reaching for an ashtray,

nothing in his notebook
but this. Nobody knows him. There is nothing

~~waiting. The twin barmen~~
~~serve him with their backs to one another.~~

~~waiting. And the barman's~~
~~bewildered by his own words on a blackboard~~

~~waiting, but the barman~~

AN OLD MAN SAYING

That told it.
That's not going to waste your precious time again, is it.

Obliterate it. Nothing
there now, nothing

new for the world to hear this morning. Look
what a mess the young man's made of his new book.

I wasn't meant to be watching. But I was watching.
I was watching

that pen of his just hovering in the air
then dabbing here and there

a little shape or two, then a cross, a swoop,
why not then it's up, up

and away am I bothering you?
He turns away with a grin. Am I bothering you,

sir? Now he's pretending I'm not here.
Of course, he's a writer, nobody else is here.

Raul a man of the arts
has gotten in here somehow, a smoking man of the arts

here, here you can have a light
from a stranger, a light

between strangers, here:
there.

You must not
ashtray Raul, you must not

let yourself be distracted by this old
barfly. You must drink your beer ice cold

like an all-American boy and write your all-
important works of verse. *Ashtray Raul*

so the poet can be left
to his shift. To his shift,

ssh, the all-important Saturday
afternoon poetry shift. Today's the day

to cross it out.
Today's the day, I'm standing up, the day to cross it out.

And I
make no appearance in the work of art. I

wander to the window, *see Raul is he writing*
'Joe wanders to the window . . .' *Is he writing*

'Finishing off his whisky, Joe rises
and weaves his way towards the angelic faces

in the golden light
of autumn and remembers to turn right

through the sunbeams
to his last final destination which seems

to be a bathroom. *God be with you Joey
I too am with you Joey . . .'*

unquote did you hear that
sir, now I'm the poet,

quote unquote, I'm the poet.
And the poet

now he's just sitting trying to pretend I've gone
with his poetry pen kind of hovering over the next one:

'I say, the drunken chap has now departed
the scene, what-ho, good egg.' Go on, get started.

He didn't know I know he's an English gent.
Warm the beer, Raul, there's an English gent

on duty.
This door won't open again. An English gent on duty.

RAUL CHALKING UP SPECIALS

Don't worry, guy, that's Joe. Joe's got issues.
He thinks you're sitting in his spot. Stay there,
guy, what are you crazy, you paid money
to sit, you don't buy tickets for the barstool.
Another Bass? It's kind of he's like a fixture.
(Is that how you spell *asparagas*? It's not . . .

with a *u*? That can't be right. You sure that's not
some British thing? Okay.) No Joe's got issues.
(No way. It's on the house.) Joe was a fixture
way before my time. He was sitting there
the day I started. I give you the Barstool
of Joey Stone! We ought to charge some money

jeezus. (*Fennal.*) Charge some freakin money.
(With an *e*? You're shittin me. It is? No it's not.)
But hey you're sitting on Joey Stone's Own Barstool
so I got to believe you, right? Him and his issues.
And he sits there sure, but he also sits over there,
in the window staring, talk about a fixture

he sits there, he's a lookout, that's a fixture
of this establishment. People pay good money
to watch him sitting there. If he's sitting there
it's a normal day in the city! And if he's not,
let's not go there . . . Hey Joe, you got some issues
need the window treatment? This is the Barstool

of, what's your name? Of . . . *Clint?* This is the Barstool
of Clint. (It's on me, Clint.) No Joe's a fixture.
Yep. And you know, *he's* British. He's got issues
of Britishness. He saw your British money,
you notice that? Just been there? But he's not —
I mean you wouldn't know, right? *You cool there,*

Joe? He's one of you but he won't go there.
Another old guy wanting the same barstool.
Same place you're headed, right? Like it or not.
Open your eyes one day and you're a fixture,
sure, and you got a tab instead of money,
and a kid sits in your spot and you got issues,

then you're a fixture too. *You sleeping there,*
Joe? Got sleeping issues. At least the barstool
keeps him awake. (I'm not gonna take your money!)

GRANNY MAY ON THE STAIRS

Joey, Joey come down. I won't come up.
    I got some tea made, dear.
    Don't make me troop up there
With all my troubles, Joey, every step's
    A trial to me.

Joey, I seen the smoke, is all it is.
    I know, it's Hermit Road.
    You knew it was near, you said.
You know somebody there, is it the milk boys?
    Who then. Poor dabs.

That was the thump you said. I got tea made
    Downstairs, oh my blessed back
    I swear. Let's have a look.
That would be 38 if it was *this* street.
    38 and 40.

If it was *this* street it would be the Stacks.
    The Stacks and who? Is that right?
    The Luscoms. What a sight.
It's like a dream where everybody wakes
    And all of the whole world's . . .

I don't mean a dream. Don't let your tea go cold,
    Joey. I told your mum
    We would be all the same
Come what may! Because there's been some killed
    God rest their souls

And us still here. I won't have it go to waste,
    Joey. I'm going down.
    Can't save every one.
I'll fetch it up. My Sunday my day of rest,
    My God. That wasn't swearing,

Joey now, that was a morning prayer,
    all there was time for. Well,
    RAW MATERIAL
IS WAR MATERIAL, I read that somewhere.
    Where are you going, dear?

Don't go there, Joey! The blinkin world's on fire.
    There's nothing to bring back.
    What do you mean 'to look'?
There's unexploded! Joey! It's the war
    That's all, it's the blessed war.

MAN IN A LITTLE FLOWERBED

It's started, can't you see son, it's the flaming
start of it it's the gasworks you can flaming
see from here it's the Thames Board, it's Loders,
it's Tate and Lyle, that's Tate and Lyle, that's Loders,
that's the Thames Board, this whole bed of roses
is my own work and my wife's this bed of roses
and now I'm standing in it she'd tell me off
for standing in it a right royal telling off
I'd cop from Stella. Who? The Prays and the Pipers
since you inquire. The Prays and the Pipers. The Pipers
I mean have a butcher's *sunshine,* wiped out
there's fuck all where there was before. Wiped out
Bob Piper he had Glenlivet. There's them Prays
in the road. Lucky name that Prays, as in God prays
it's them ones. Look at the soil all over these shoes.
Look at the soil all over these two good shoes.
Better do something quick. That's Betsy Pray
holding the littl'un, holding the littlest Pray.
Only a baby, eye of the storm she's like.
The girlies made it through, and them lads. It looks like
everybody. In night attire! Nine lives
them hooligans I always go, nine lives.
Eight lives now. Old man he's a firewatcher,
Arthur Pray, somewhere. *I'm* a firewatcher!
Morning, vicar, see that? Tate and Lyle's,
stone the flaming crows that's Tate and Lyle's,
one lump or two? Don't think so! Look at them Prays
lost everything. Everyone knows them Prays.
Up and down like billy-o of a springtime

evening on them bikes. I like the springtime
personally. That's Harry, piece of my mind
I gave him once, he's a good lad, he don't mind.
Look at him digging away. Ain't got no stuff.
Wish I could give 'em my stuff but it's my own stuff
more's the pity. Now Robby, he don't care.
Keeps his eye on the doughnut. He don't care
who suffers for it. House to house he'll go.
Cooking up something are we I always go.
Look at the blonde, that's Sally, one lump or two,
don't mind if I do, with that one, tea for two
at an hotel of her choosing! Then there's the ghost girl.
Give her a blanket for crying out loud the ghost girl.

HARRY PRAY IN HIS COAT

Something like five o'clock.
    I kept them in my sights.
I saw the last few turning back.
    They were probably Messerschmitts.

One brilliant thing there was
    Was over the south-southeast
In the teeth of it. There were these pink flares
    Exploding with this sort of gust

Of silent light, then you'd hear it.
    Search me what they were.
Of course our sisters couldn't bear it,
    Could you, stuck in there.

Godsend, our little hole, mind,
    Godsend. See, Joe.
Everything's buried in a mound
    But us. We're going to have to go

When Dad comes. But where?
    I suppose we're 'refugees'.
World's our oyster, Joey. Here,
    Help me with these.

ROBBY PRAY TAKING OFF HIS GAS MASK

Look who it isn't. If it isn't the ice cream man!
Morning, ice cream man.
You come to sell ice cream to the survivors
Joey? Or is it *Giuseppe*? Or *Jew*-seppy?
That'll be chocolate for Harry, chocolate for me,
strawberry for our mum,
Jew-seppy, where's *your* mum?
Here's our mum, where's your mum?
Or should I say your *mama*, your *mama mia*?
Where's your *mama mia*, ice cream man?
I'm only telling him, Mum. He *is* an eye-tie.
His dad's not an eye-tie but his mum's an eye-tie,
that's why she's buggered off cos she's in hiding,
isn't she, Jew-seppy?
Did I finish taking the order? Vanilla for Sal.
Only the best mind you. Same for the baby.
Nuts for Julie, got any nuts, Jew-seppy?
Nuts for her. I'm always teasing my sister.
Look at me, won't you Julie? She's struck dumb.
Nothing to do with the bomb.
Sight of the ice cream man in all his glory.
Can you tell your mum,
Joey, Joey-oni, can you tell your mum
we're all still here? Will you do that, Joey-oni?
Putting my mask back on.
Funniest feeling something don't belong.

SALLY PRAY ON THE KERB

Everyone's come to look at where we were.
There's nothing to see, though, is there, Julie. There,
there. I say it to you but you're not crying
    I'm the one.

You're the one not doing a single thing
but looking at your fingers, I'm the one.
Everyone's come to look at our old home
    when it's too late

for visits. Should have been there yesterday.
Given you lemonade we did have plenty.
Didn't think I'd cry, it's not as if I'm
    at the pictures,

it's just I loved that house it's never sunk in.
It never has. Mrs Piper, she was digging
yesterday and she said for Victory
    poor old Jule.

Look, there's Joey Stone. I knew he'd come.
Nothing's happened to him. I had this dream.
There's the silver balloons, are they just there
    to say hello?

Halloo, silver balloons. Can you lift us up
and put us down in a bluebell field of sheep
high in the mountains? We want to hitch a ride,
    me and my sis,

if that's your destination. What did you say?
What did you say there, Jule? The Crystal County?
You heard her. The Crystal County, silver balloons,
    at the double!

BETSY PRAY LOOKING SOUTH

There's six they set for Arthur now there's
Six new fires

To mind there ain't no way of knowing
Which it is

He's working at but Arthur that's
For him to know

It's war work he can't say you kids
When he comes home

When he comes home well home she goes
Just look at it

It's if you cry it goes zigzagged
All the world

Splatters all ways and Sally what's with
Julie why

She only saying jingles give
The girl a shake

Enough to say she had it's only
Yesterday

I had the wireless on I had
Some classical

Geraldo and His Orchestra it's
Soft I go

Turn the wireless up there Harry
Can't he goes

It's everything that's coming
It's begun he goes

Sky's chocker with them sort of like
A ticker tape

Bandwagon's on I say I shall not
Move an inch

For anyone not *that* man nor no
Ticker tape

JULIE PRAY LOOKING AT HER FINGERS

lantern	*crookback*	*lodger*	*sly*
lantern	*crookback*	*lodger*	*sly*
lantern	*I can*	*see for*	*miles*

lantern	*crookback*	*lodger*	*sly*
crookback	*I'm my*	*only*	*hope*
crookback	*lantern*	*lodger*	*sly*

crookback	*crookback*	*crookback*	*crookback*
lodger	*I don't*	*know my*	*strength*
sly	*sly*	*sly*	*sly*

sly

sly

sly

sly

ssssshhhhhhhhhhh

RAUL EMPTYING ASHTRAYS

The guy's asleep, are you done, you British guys?
Are you done contributing?
Do we what, do we go on alone?
Is it time now?

I'm kidding. Give us a signal, give us a sign!
Give us the thumbs-up, Joey.
He's out of it, I tell you.
Hey Brits,

You want us to save your ass again? You guys
You nap, we'll take the watch.
We'll wake you for the next one,
Are you in?

I'm kidding with you Clint. Clint can take it,
Clint's smiling in his beer.
He's thinking *this dumbass!*
Or is it *arse*?

He's thinking *this silly arse!* Hey Joe you with us?
It's the middle of next week!
Easy now, it's okay,
It's Saturday

Still, and it's still, or it was, an awesome day.
The ladies are gone though Joey.
Clint scared them off with some poems,
You missed it all!

JOEY AWAKE NOW

Some poems,
right some poems.

I'm a lover of poems.
And yes, we lovers of poems

must stick together. Don't mind me. Pardon? Glenn?
Glenn? Glenn. It is nice to meet you, Glenn.

You are thinking you are in luck.
Because look,

a strange old man has joined you at the bar.
How fortunate you are

this fine day. I beg your pardon? Indeed.
The secret's out. I am indeed

a man with English, how do you say Raul, *issues,*
exactly, English *issues.*

No, not for fifty years.
Hoboken Italian now for fifty years.

I'm English when there are wars.
I was English when there were wars.

Oh no you don't have to pretend
you give a damn. You came here to write, my friend,

then a sleepy old fool comes dropping by to tell you
what it was like in *his* day. Well I'll tell you:

I was extremely handsome. It took me
seconds to go to the bathroom. End of story.

Raul, the same for him and the same for me,
he's being much too polite. English, you see,

not like us. I'd have said Bugger off
by now. Raul doesn't get that, 'bugger off'

he thinks it's some kind of cool
new vodka, don't you, Raul?

Raul says he understands,
he understands

bugger off
it's what I was afraid of,

no secrets now, no secrets
for the Brits,

not from Americans
Glenn, no secrets from Americans.

The war?
Ah-ha.

Look at him, pen at the ready, like I could say
some poetry. We lovers of poetry.

What's so important in the world that you can't
stop the ride a moment,

open a little black
empty book

and remind the world you're blue? There's not a thing.
Burning building? Nothing.

Love of a lady?
'I am at work. Please ask her to wait in the lobby.'

His eyes are glazing over, he's remembering
something he's forgetting

something. If you ask me, to tell you,
Glenn, if you're sincerely truly going to,

I may
do so. I may

tell you a thing or two, I wouldn't do so,
I wouldn't — *muchas gracias* — I wouldn't do so,

only it's Saturday.
Not Saturday,

Black Saturday.
And in sixty years of rinso white Saturdays

it never did find
one to hide behind.

You go through morning into afternoon
and it's always sunny, Saturday, in rain

or snow or storm who cares?
you pass the hours,

you're free and the crowd is free and the whistle blows
a goal is scored, the long shot by a nose

then you happen to glance at the sky
and I say you I mean *I* . . .

I say you I mean *I, me*
riding on my bike and I

saw this mass of planes
in patterns they were their planes

and with the sky so thick
the light was weak, your hold on it was weak

your life so far
some kind of lucky break. They were everywhere

and in the day,
not in the night in the day like your worst fear suddenly

figured it out and came.
What's stopping us? I rode my bike straight home

to tell my gran and I'm pedalling for my life
I know they can see me up there! *Hey Ralf*

shoot zat paper boy or he'll never stop!
Never stop

telling ze vorld on us . . .
Raul's laughing at me. *You're not?* That's how it was.

Personal, kind of. Felt you were in their minds.
They were in our minds,

pale types, munching schnitzel! Here
well it's true they had the Japs but not *here,*

they didn't have them out of a blue sky
over the skyline on a Saturday.

September 7th. What do you mean it's the 8th?
The Saturday was the 7th, it wasn't the 8th.

He's telling *me.* Where do you come from? Pardon?
Say again what garden? Well-in-the-Garden?

Oh there.
Shredded Wheat's made there.

That was the sort of place we thought we'd get to.
Because we had to get to

somewhere, we were bombed out
on the first night of the thing. Or, we weren't bombed out

precisely, me and my gran,
she always believed what I told her, did my gran,

Mrs Katherine Mabel Stone.
Truth of the matter is, I had my own

reason for getting out.
It isn't a thing you know when it's happening. But

you're young,
you're wearing a wedding ring,

we figure it out in time.
You'll understand how it was if you give a damn.

And if you don't give a damn it'll still be there
a year or so anywhere

you find me. Soon I won't be giving one either.
Then you and I can give not a damn forever.

MAN GETTING OFF A BIKE

I'm telling you I saw him he was crying!
He came here it was secret, it was secret he was crying
  He was going all round everywhere
He was on our spot of earth
  With his hat and his havana
It's on my breath!

He was bigger than his pictures he was weeping.
It was a secret visit, but he wouldn't make a secret
  Of his weeping, that was public
And he nearly set me off
  It's been buggered with the traffic
And I've said enough

So you can shine a light and ask me questions:
It shall remain a secret. And as for their next location
  You can twist me like a corkscrew
I ain't saying what I know!
  He asks are we downhearted
And we all go *NO!*

Or, if you read about it in the future,
That someone shouted out to him 'It's good of you to visit!
  We can take it, give it back to 'em!'
That man's identity
  Is secret till the end of time
But—confidentially . . .

HARRY SALVAGING THINGS

He knows he's crossed the line.
       He knows what he's just done,
Joe, I shouldn't like to be
       Civilians in Berlin

Right now, he broke the rules.
       Or civilians in Rome,
Robby true but Joe grew up here
       Here's his home.

Here was ours. Good God.
       Fits in a ruddy cart.
Anyone have any bright ideas
       Concerning what

Exactly happens now?
       I didn't think so. Right,
No point in standing looking at it
       Day and night

Until the next one comes.
       Ever wondered how
It feels on the front line, anyone?
       Don't have to now.

GRANNY MAY AT THE SCENE

I thought I'd lost you, Joey, who are these
    All over everywhere
    Don't stand and stare
At her she's had a shock, look at her eyes.

Thought you'd joined the navy like your dad
    I did just then I thought
    He's off to war I ought
To stop him he's too young I said I prayed

I weren't too late, I asked the Lord a favour.
    Won't say what I said
    I'd do for Him instead.
Only I'll have to do it now and I'd rather

See your dad come home again. What's done.
    That stretcher's coming out
    That lady's put a sheet
Where someone ought to be and you're too young

To look at it. That house it's disappeared.
    A thing like that can't just
    Happen, Joey, the rest
All spared. Look at her hand, she wasn't spared.

Cover it up, that's right, they must have been
    Spies or something Joe.
    Must have been in the know.
Hitler must have thought they knew his plan.

You don't know anything, do you Joey? That's good.
    Better safe than sorry.
    The King he's in a fury,
He's hopping mad, won't stand for it I heard.

Don't know about madame. Don't know for sure
    She knows it's started, her.
    What's that sound, m'dear,
What's a-rattling me diamond cup and saucer . . .

Let's get away now Joey, leave 'em be,
    Poor dabs. They didn't know.
    These days you never know
Who's moving in next door, next thing you see

They're carrying 'em out. Look at the sky.
    You say that's what they are
    Them circles way up there
I call them angel circles up so high.

ROBBY IN HIS GAS MASK

Repeat. Repeat. All foreigners at once
to channel ports.
All Germans keep on walking till the water's
so high then keep walking till it's so high
then so high
then so high and so on glug glug nice helmet.

Repeat. Repeat. All foreigners at once
to channel ports.
Italians yes we know you're scared of water
you're scared of everything so you just stroll
along this path
that takes you up this really charming White Cliff,

then face the Continong and proceed forwards.
What's that Harry?
He's right, I forget you never heard of forwards.
Turn and proceed backwards till you notice
you're in mid-air.
Then assemble on the beach in a dead fashion.

I'm always teasing him it's just my manner.
It's not as if
he's German if he was you see that lamppost?
We're in a scrap, you got to make a choice.
Not a choc-ice
Joey, a choice, what can I do with you?

SALLY TYING HER SISTER'S SHOE

There's Joey Stone.
        Joey we have to
say goodbye.
Because we've nothing
        see that zero
in the sky?

No aeroplane
        did that it's too
good to be true.
They're sending us
        away somewhere
we won't have you

delivering
        our paper no one
will at all.
Because it's Nowhere-
        shire because it's
Nowhere Hall.

Will you still bring
        a paper to
the ruins Joe?
Say you will
        no need to
but say so.

HOME GUARD MAN BREATHLESS

Toffee Mile more like. I saw these lads
with chisels coming back, it makes no sense
the way they look, they're coming back with spades
and chisels coming back
            and their bloody hands

are black from what on earth is that I go
and Gibb from Beckton says the Sugar Mile
is burning, boys and girls, the world's aglow
this Gibb from Beckton says
            with Tate and Lyle's

finest dark selection. I say right,
has anyone told the police? But by the time
the words are out they're words to be laughed at
Has anyone tewld the police
            habout this hawful crame!

I let them pass right by, I keep my cool.
There's hundreds walking out of Silvertown
and someone said they're headed for a school.
Hundreds walking out
            in shock from Silvertown

today have you heard anything? You've not.
I want some toffee too with my Jenny near me.
Sun has the nerve to shine and with no hat.
I want dark toffee too.
            No one can hear me.

GRANNY MAY AMONG MANY

Dozed off I must have done when they decided
    That if two souls are safe
    Like you Joe and myself

They ought to squash their home into a barrow.
    Or if the street they know
    And came to years ago

Looks just the same as always they should leave it.
    And if they can smell smoke
    That's fit to make you puke

You trot towards it taking a deep breath,
    So you can sing a song
    The same as everyone

Of how there'll always be what fools can see
    There'll never be again.
    Blind women and blind men

Following a painted line. On Braid Street
    It was very plain to see
    Rats went the other way

But who am I. Dozed off I must have done
    When this was voted on
    Somewhere by everyone.

JOEY FOLDING THE *NEW YORK TIMES*

No. You can think a person who would be now
a hundred and thirty died before their time.
You think they should live, now.

You can if you loved that person, you can if you're how
or why that person, what am I saying . . . I'm
past mine, my time.

Wouldn't have thought I'd ever write the year
2000 . . . 2001! Doesn't look right.
Looks more like the year

aliens land, with all those zeroes there
like faces, and this 1 . . . it looks like what?
Beginning all over. Right,

when what's to begin again? I inform the Lord
I can't get any slower, I can't get
stiller than this for the Lord

to hold me in His cross hairs. People thought
in the war the things they hit were precisely what
they aimed for. I forget

where I read that they were accidents, the bombs,
technically speaking, accidents. They just
glanced and let the bombs

loose where they saw fire. I did have dreams
I was a gunner hurtling from the east
in a Heinkel and I just

press, and I see the U-bend of the Thames
so jolly and blue below. And I'm aware
that someone near the Thames

is strolling, then I'm him too in the dreams,
looking up, considering a prayer.
But as I say *aware.*

JOEY AFTER A WHILE

And so we came to this school on Agate Street
in Canning Town, it was late

we were dead beat
a man rides by repeating *Yellow alert*

Yellow alert.
Point is, we had no right but the way I saw it

anyone had the right.
Purple alert

he goes. *You're like a rainbow* says Gran
and he storms off on his bike, somebody's son.

I knew this family.
They had an old name and the name was Pray.

They were bombed out and the older sister Sally
kindly did inform me

this school in Canning Town
would hold them all for now. They were sending down

transport, the Ministry
was sending three, always that number, three,

three
coaches due to arrive there when? At three!

God's honest truth that Sunday afternoon.
You wait an hour for a bus, we Englishmen

are telling an English joke here Raul I'm afraid
you won't understand, you need some kind of card

not a green card,
a pink card,

where was I?
There was, there was activity in the sky

by now, we weren't sure whose
and Gran had ceased to care, her only shoes

were hopeless and I wheeled her in the barrow,
I wheeled that lady in the blessed barrow

Lord. The ARP man comes again
and Gran inquires what colour but the siren

ruins his big line.
I wheel her up to the gate and it's three-fifteen

and of course I think too late! but I see no bus.
Let alone three. There's a warden bawling at us

Take cover! and I ask where.
So he lets us through without the questionnaire

he'd hoped to give us, and as we pass the gate
we pass a sign some fellow's painted white,

white words on a white
sign, but if you look you can make it out

SOUTH HALLSVILLE
SCHOOL

Agate
Street

HARRY FOLDING HIS COAT

There, one luxury pillow
    For Sally and one for Jule.
Robby's speechless, having to spend
    Sunday in Sunday school.

We played this lot last year.
    I made a goal. So I hope
No one recognises me,
    We could get roughed up!

Robert look bloody help.
    Mum's shot to pieces. Here,
You people, this is the Pray domain
    From this chair to that chair.

Make yourselves at home.
    Make yourselves our home!
Make yourselves a castle
    Till the buses come.

It isn't going to be bad.
    You expected a London bus
To arrive on time, you must be nuts!
    There's water and there's gas

And we're not in that corridor.
    They stuck the Fouchers there.
Let's give them all a wave. Evening.
    Imagine us being here.

CHIEF WARDEN ON A CLOAKROOM BENCH

You claim you are J. L. Stone and K. M. Stone
of Silvertown. I am writing it with this pen
and passing the badges over to be worn
      at all times.

We fully expect the transport by the onset
of nightfall which we do anticipate
is soon. The presumption being it took a route
      that took some time.

Space is of course at a premium. The room
to your right I have commandeered for 'a powder room'
given the circumstances, while this cloakroom
      at this time

is the Operations Hub. Now in addition
we are assured there will exist provision
for foodstuffs and the like at this location
      in a short time

to be determined. Whom did you say? The Prays?
I now consult the document. *The Prays* . . .
Name: Mrs E. L. Pray. There are several Prays,
      and in their *Time*

column I read 2:20. They are five
in number, plus an infant. I believe
they were among the first ones to arrive
      and for the time

being classroom seven is their abode.
Down the corridor, careful where you tread,
right at the end. We'll have you on the road
in no time.

SALLY CURLING UP WITH JULIE

Only me and you — is it you and me? —
only you and me
    know

that only you and me — no it's you and I —
only you and I
    know

only the big balloons up there so high
you want to cry
    know

what's in your mind and that's why they're on a string!
They're listening,
    no

we're listening and that's why we're so quiet.
I'm not quiet
    no

you're quiet. Because you're seeing what they see,
so you know what they
    know.

ROBBY CROSS-LEGGED

Too late, Harry, he's seen us.
Ice cream man and his granny. That about tops it
really, know what I mean. Nice day, Robby?
Yeah, not bad. Got bombed to buggery. Sorry.
Got bombed to Germany. Sorry, can't stop swearing.
Got bombed, got rags to wear,
walked for miles and now it's a bleedin schoolday.
Nice and comfy, pocketed a Woodbine,
future reference, and I spot Jew-seppy,
ice cream purveyor extraordinaire who's only
trotted backwards all the livelong way
from Ice Cream Land to be with us, it's touching.

Where's my choc-ice, Joey?
Where's my sister's Sno-creme, we're hungry.
We're the hungry race of English.
Give him a little room, the ice cream man,
he can set up his sugar machine and his ice machine
and his who knows what, all of his dark trade secrets.
Get bombed yourself? You liar.
Give the liar some leg room.
You here for the great school trip, Pinocchio?
Where's your Pinocchio gas mask?
Lily's got Mickey Mouse, it's got ears.
They don't do a one for liars.

BETSY STANDING UP

Have you seen them buses, Joseph, have you
Seen them buses

What do they say we do for money
Tell me someone

Take her oh she's oh she's soaking
Sally take her

Look at our Julie staring at her
Bleedin fingers

Rob, ask Joseph ask him has he
Seen them buses

Albie Rogers, he's the only
Bloke that's in here

Harry, is that Albie Rogers
Is that Albie

In here but he's got no children
Why's he in here

Harry ask him why he ain't out
Fighting fires with

Arthur. Why's it rude. You ask him
Ask him Robby

CHIEF WARDEN ON A TRESTLE TABLE

I am informed may I reiterate
I am informed by bicycle the transport
departed from the depot too late

to manifest itself before nightfall
at this location. Please. Therefore meanwhile
we shall appropriate this present school,

anonymous by dint of regulations,
for a night shelter. Please. I shall take questions
in due course at the Hub of Operations

which you may find between the 'Fairy' cloakroom
and the 'Pixie' cloakroom (to employ the peacetime
school nomenclature). Please keep your classroom

smart. We will establish a kitchen station
behind this signpost bearing the word KITCHEN
in orange writing. Tea and hot stew madam

since you inquire we have no sugar please!
Service shall be by classroom number please!
All in good time ladies please please ladies!

JOEY LIGHTING UP

My gran, my Granny May,
had found a friend of hers in classroom three,

so I settled Gran down comfortably with her,
and I said I'm going in there,

Gran, I can see the Prays of Hermit Road.
And the Prays of Hermit Road,

Harry, Robby, Sally, Julie,
and the baby's name was Lily

I do believe, of course were why I'd come.
We weren't bombed out like them.

I was only young,
but it was all hands to the pumps, and there were some

were probably thinking why's that lad in here?
But the Prays, they knew this man there was in there,

no wife or kids, *Rogers,* he swore blind
he wasn't Rogers, swore his name was *Medland,*

said he'd lost his daughter.
Either way the man had no daughter.

Everyone was shattered, dead beat,
dead still on their feet.

It was what, it was the changes,
it was the sky, it was jagged edges

everywhere, the stink from the docks on fire.
If people were going somewhere you went there.

And Gran went
where I went

and I went
where my heart I suppose I went where my heart went.

Ahem, he goes, ahem.
Observes me from the brim

of his ice-cold beer does Glenn,
the breakfast cereal gentleman,

sees them lighting fire after fire,
someone on the white cliffs up here

in the dark in the Stone brain
making the chain again,

sixty-one little fires in the dark, September
to September.

RAUL AT HAPPY HOUR

I swear you guys are keeping us in business.
What is it with you Brits, you ruled the world
one time, how did you do that *drunk*? I tell you,
you know it's our turn now, but we don't do that.
We walk the thin white line, you ought to try it.
You lovely ladies gonna need ID.

I said you ladies gonna need ID.
You're Britney freakin Spears, I'm out of business
if I serve you. Here, Joey, you should try it,
waking up some morning in the world
all kind of clean inside? Only don't do that
while I'm still working here. Hey, I tell you,

and don't you say a word if I do tell you
you Brits — *hey Love-of-my-life, this your ID?*
Like twelve she looks. Fourteen tops. Check that.
She's legal, or some guy in the forgery business
We Salute You. *Rum? What a wicked world.*
Sweetheart, you're gonna suffer. Okay try it.

Clint I might be leaving. *Go on try it.*
Moving on up, I feel I ought to tell you.
Wasn't so shabby. Gotta go up in the world
of catering or — *guys, need to see ID —*
you're fucked excuse my language. That's the business.
It's in the nature. So, I'm waiting on that,

this offer. In the meantime this and that.
If ever I see a way you know I try it,
always I do. If it's pleasure, or it's business,
always jump, don't stand there. Was that you,
Joey, way back when? Can I see ID,
Mr Stone, I'm kidding! No that's my world.

Keep moving you can *move* the goddamn world!
Stand still, you wanna stand still, you *do* that—
you lovely ladies gonna need ID —
nothing comes of nothing. Gotta try it,
right? — *hey I'm from Cleveland like you,*
Cheyenne, you married? What? It's all my business! —

I have to try it on, you know, in my world.
'Mind your own damn business.' You hear that?
Your ID, kid, is *way* hotter than you.

II

CHIEF WARDEN ATOP A PIANO

I should like to take this opportunity
everyone to wish you all good morning.
Good morning.

I am informed by bicycle the transport
is scheduled to depart the transport depot
at eleven hundred hours, that's

eleven hundred hours, which is to say
this very morning. Please. Thank you.
A Monday, not a Sunday,

a Monday morning service of thanksgiving
will take place in the corridor between
classrooms seven and nine

in the peacetime designation. (This is unstable.)
At nine. Nine hundred hours. (I haven't marked it,
I was extremely careful.)

Further announcements will be made — beg pardon?
A question from the floor . . . Well as it happens
I can, son, yes I can.

Young gentleman's inquiring as to whether
I myself do play the pianoforte
(if I might just climb down . . .)

to which the answer is as it happens I do.
Well now we have some hush. I expect you know
this little one about bluebirds?

RAUL SERVING SUNDAY BRUNCH

Hey. Enjoy. See Joey found the sunshine,
it got him. Land of Nod.
That'll be you there, Clint,
give it a year

that'll be you in the window dead to the world,
I tell you. What does he do?
Nothing, he's old, he's done.
He's just Joey.

Said he was with FedEx or UPS
some postal deal. He did well.
You know as much as I do,
hell. More.

You getting the old war story? You Brits,
still fighting the German guys,
like Mr Fawlty, right? That
cracks me up.

*

One time I say my brother's a marine.
Joey says merchant marine?
And I'm like, a *merchant* marine?
No a marine.

Joey was in the merchant marines and I'm like,
what *is* a merchant marine?
Sounds like you sell people shit
then kick their ass.

Is that the thing with the empire? Hey I cracked it,
Clint, that's how you guys
did it, you sold people shit
then kicked their ass.

There's a *U.S.* merchant marine? You're shittin me.
Sign me up I tell you.
That's a million bucks to you
mi amigo

and meanwhile put your fucking hands up. Cool.
Merchant marines rule.
Catering corps I guess I'm
catering corps.

*

Married a couple times he did say once.
Last one died about
three years four years five years?
Anyway.

*

I'm waiting on the phone. I got this offer
did I tell you, keep it quiet,
I'm waiting for the call.
Good money.

*

Thing is he's an old guy and he forgets,
that's all he isn't senile
no way the guy's just old,
loses the plot.

He ought to remember you from yesterday.
I mean you guys were close,
you're buddies, what are you
you're *blokes,*

you got your British issues, got that style.
Old, young, or, you know,
like you, it's that royal style
shaken not stirred

you know what I'm saying. I mean we could care less
what's happening with you guys
but whatever it is
it's classy.

Also, you come in here and you're from London.
From where? . . . Right. From London.
And you know it's an Irish bar
there's an Irish flag

flying there but you're cool. This is New York.
Whatever you guys have done,
whoever's right or wrong
you walk in here

you're in America. We don't judge. Some guy
kicks it off I'm Raul.
I kick his ass, merchant
marine style.

*

I was gonna say there's something Joey brought
this morning. See the yellow
envelope in his lap?
Watch out

it's the life story. I know what he's going to ask you.
Great writer Joseph Stone
suddenly discovered
at seventy-something

sleeping in an Irish joint on Broadway.
He's holding it pretty tight
even in his dreams,
old merchant marine.

MR ALBIE ROGERS

What are you looking at me for? I don't know you. I'm
here, I'm here the same as everyone else is here. Your boys
keep looking at me. That's not my name. I've never heard
of any Albie Roberts. Albie Rogers you say. Same difference.
Never heard of him. My name . . . is Medland.

Dennis Medland and I've lost my daughter. Since you ask.
My daughter's four and I've lost her I can't find her. Since
you ask. I've not seen her since it hit. Know what that's
like? I see you have kids yourself but none of them are
missing. Mine are, mine is. What's her name? Her name? Is
Mary.

ROBBY BACK FROM THE PLAYGROUND

The gross hand's on the zwolf.
And the klein hand's on the zwolf.
And there's absolutely sod all out there
see for yourself.

SALLY DEALING CARDS

First thing we're going to do when we arrive
is go out to the farthest field they have,
Julie and me whatever the farmer says
and lie there till there's nothing there but stars.

And in the morning helping out his lads
feeding the pigs and whatnot in the pig yards
that'll be very tiring so we'll swim
after it's done we'll have a communal swim.

Lunch will be outside if it's this warm
on a gigantic table made of hornbeam
and I shall pass the oranges to Jack
I've named him and he'll give me a little kick

nobody notices. After the washing up
we ride our cycles to the village shop
for sweet supplies. Julie will start to talk
and she'll still be yakking on on our evening walk

to this stream that's got five swans. That's how far
I've thought ahead. It isn't all that far.
Not every day will be the same as that
and every time I think of it it changes.

CHIEF WARDEN LADLING STEW

I know no more than you, sir. I was informed
by bicycle sixteen hundred hours.
Not thirteen hundred sixteen hundred. No.
Sixteen hundred. The prior information
of thirteen hundred hours is superseded
by sixteen hundred. (That is to say, young lady,
four o'clock. Of course you knew. Smart girl.)

In answer to your earlier question, ma'am,
a gentleman who signed himself *D. Medland*
arrived here yesterday. I'm afraid it's outside
my remit whether or not it's his real name.

No, we have no *A. Rogers*. We have no *Rogers*.
He signed himself *D. Medland* he's *D. Medland*.

That's as may be, ma'am. Hundreds have come here
homeless, without formal documentation.
The Ministry will address that in due course
but meanwhile the priority remains
evacuation from the zone of London.

Whether it's Rogers or bloody Rumpelstiltskin.

BETSY ROCKING THE BABY

What do we want the country for there's
Nothing there

Everything we had is where it's
Always been

They wouldn't let us dig they wouldn't
Let us wait

How's Arthur going to find us when
His shift is done

Fine coming home that is fine coming
Home that is

Smell bacon can't you frying it's them
Classroom five

They're getting special treatment getting
Benefits

They had a truck they did, they wouldn't
Let us pass

Not even with a by your leave. I've
Half a mind

To speak to him. I've half a mind to
Raise my voice

Only I'll wake you won't I Lily
Dreamalong

Dreamalong to market in your
Market shoes

They had a truck they did I know they
Let them dig

I've half a mind to ask them what I've
Half a mind

To say is not for your ears little
Dreamalong

Sandman's at the window time to
Shut your eyes

They wouldn't let us dig we never
Had the things

They had so they don't know fine coming
Home that is

Where's he to find us nothing's got a
Sign no more

It's all gone white and where's a bloke to
Hang a raincoat

'MR DENNIS MEDLAND'

No I don't live on Hermit Road I've never heard of Hermit
Road. So what if you do I don't. I live on . . . Middle Road.
Number 67. So what if you haven't heard of it I was happy
there. So were we all. Mary and me, Mary and us.

I came here when it hit because they told me everything
was dangerous and everyone was coming here to a shelter,
to a school, to this school for children.

My daughter Mary's school in fact, a school known to me
prior, which is quite a matter of chance.

Why don't you boys, now you have this unlikely holiday,
instead of looking at me like you know me, look out of the
window there, where all you see's blue sky and a fluffy
white passing cloud. And a fluffy white passing vapour trail
that's probably one of Adolf's. It's that man again, we can
see him, he can see us. Spotted any bluebirds? Well.
Neither have I. Neither have I and I'm a man with eagle
eyes.

HARRY DEALING CARDS

Put it this way. If I had a suitcase
I'd open it and I might iron my shirt
but I certainly wouldn't put my socks in drawers
    because unlike you kids

I can't be wasting time on a ruddy farm
at my age. Have to do my bit. Eighteen
in April don't forget. I'll stay a night
    and eat a roast with you

and get you settled down. When you next see me
I'll be in uniform. I'm not sure which.
I may well have a beard. Why is that funny?
    All very well laughing

when it's summer all year long. Not in the service.
Our lads are copping it every night and day
over our heads right now, don't you forget it,
    kiddies. Spades are trumps.

ROBBY STRETCHING HIS LEGS

First thing I'm gonna do is swipe a car
and get myself back here. Course I can drive.
It's easy, a girl could do it. An Italian
girl could do it, couldn't you Joey? First thing.

Second thing, hook up with the Upton gang.
Do a little business, coin a phrase,
waste not want not, dig for victory
blah blah blah. Move up west. Next thing.

Next thing, well. Meet an American starlet.
They have them in their army, not starlets,
females, and their army's going to come,
I heard a rumour if we're in a hole.

This? This ain't a hole. This school's a hole
but we were just unlucky. Took a hit.
Like Mr Albie Rogers is pretending
happened to his house. And you, Jew-seppy,

what are you, vapour trail? We ain't in a hole.
Our boys'll see off Adolf. If we don't,
the stars of the United States, I tell you,
they're trained and they fight dirty, they're luscious.

GRANNY MAY AT THE KNEES-UP

Just like old times. Nothing like old times.
     I know the
        Officers' names

Joey that's Mr Varley at the keys.
      Mrs Glitzer.
        Mrs Mays.

That Laney has the voice of a nightingale.
      That's Mr
        Herbert Bull

His other leg's in Flanders he goes
      Mabel
        Mabel he goes

If you're in them parts would you take a look for me?
      Take
        A look for me

In Flanders Mabel take a look for me
      Where
        I say where

In Flanders Joey will you Joey where
      Are we
        Joey truly

SALLY PLAYING PATIENCE

It's even got a cinema
      the farmers like to go there
Joey, then they smoke cigars
      they have a film discussion
in a room with velvet fittings.

But what nobody tells them
      as nobody tells anyone
is all the famous actors
      and all the leading ladies
Robby you can think of

have also been escorted
      to the villages selected.
No one's saying much about it
      Joey but these stars
in costumes and disguises

could pass us on the meadow
      or you could be hop-picking
Joey did you ever
      and next to you right there there's
Merle Oberon, who knows,

Harry, and all the Hammers
      are operating tractors,
people with great talents
      are all to be protected
Julie for the future

so there'll still be the pictures
          to go to when it's over
and cups to play for Harry
          and parties and by that time
some of them will know us

you'll stand there with your wineglass
          you don't have to be famous
but they know you, you were there, Joey
          side by side at harvest
when stars were nothing special.

Julie, in the wheat barns
          at midnight when the work's done
anyone could stand there
          meaning what you hope's
their meaning. When it's over

everyone who went there
          will have this bond forever
and we'll bring our children out there
          in cars with silver streamlines
for the grand reunion dancing.

ROBBY BITING HIS NAILS

Think I'm just sitting here on my kingdom come?
I'm choosing my War Team,
my Cabinet, my staff.
Deputy: Harold Pray cos he knows stuff.
And taking orders from your little brother, well,
no one likes to, takes a man of class.
Minister for Information Julie.
Julia Pray, oh yes, that's got tongues wagging
on Fleet Street I can tell you. *General Pray:*
Why is our Minister of Information someone
who's lost the power of speech? Think about it, gents.
Careless talk, you with me?
Minister of Foreign Affairs . . . Jew-seppy.
A popular choice. The first of his affairs
is to remove the foreigners, then himself,
then who flippin cares.
Minister of Seams — didn't I tell you? —
thought I mentioned the Ministry of Seams.
Sally Pray. That's Lady Pray to you.
Home Office . . . well I did give this some thought
and I came up with a name not very well known
yet destined for great things.
I give you Dennis Medland or should I say
Captain Dennis Medland. He gets Home
because we ain't got a home but at the same time
he ain't Dennis Medland, so you'll agree
it's an inspired appointment.
Missing Persons Bureau: step forward
Sir Albert Rogers. Any of you seen Albie?

HARRY IN RED SUNSHINE

It's got about an inch,
    Until it drops behind
That building. It'll get cooler then
    And I shouldn't mind

If it didn't mean they're late.
    That's what I mean: later.
But it won't be dark for several hours
    It doesn't matter

Whether there's any sunshine.
    I mean there's always sunshine
If you think about it, somewhere
    In the empire at *some* time.

Did you see in the bog place,
    There are maps on every wall
You can look at while you're sitting there
    Lord of it all.

But they're all obsolete.
    They're worth about the same
As what you're doing in the bucket
    While you look at them.

JOEY THROUGH SMOKE

Christmas of '39 or January
'40 maybe. I had a paper round.
What did you do in the twentieth century

Joey? A paper round. I didn't mind
that joke they told, seeing as how it was me
who always told it first. Me and my friend

shared it, he'd do one day I'd do one day,
but that day . . . it was cold,
a frozen Sunday morning, early, frosty

all the years and I still feel that cold . . .
and my last street but one was a narrow street,
Hermit Road. Now usually I cycled

but I got a puncture so I'm on my feet,
dawdling along, a kid, you know, fifteen,
curious and I always used to read,

when I could, the daily headline news. I mean
the war was on, they called it the Bore War
as nothing much had happened. But I've seen

a movement at a window, right there,
not at the house I'm doing but along,
two or three down, house with the yellow door,

nothing's strange about that, it's just there's something
makes me look and I look and it's a girl.
It's a girl's face but veiled by the kind of netting,

you know, of the veil curtain, so it's all
misty, but her gaze, it's like a beam
and it seems to go right past me to the wall.

Where there's nothing. Well you probably assume
I'm smitten, I'm a lad, but the lad's unsure,
with those dark eyes on nothing — right beside him —

seeing! Are they, though? I'd no idea.
I stare at her, it suddenly seems I can.
I knew the name was Pray, the Prays lived there.

The father was some kind of accounts man
at Tate's. There were seven kids.
Two of them were married off, long gone

I never met them, don't know what they did.
It's another world. These days
you meet a girl you topple into bed

you take it all. Wasn't like that for us.
Had to dig deep for courage just to speak!
More than sixty years

and I'm a wreck
remembering standing on their bit of path
ready to knock . . .

I must have held my breath
so long the lad who opened the door said *Mum
there's someone here something's the matter with.*

I'm going to have that carved above my name,
I have a place in Jersey
ready for it. In fact forget the name.

Or they can still put *Joey.*
Stone, as I always say,
goes without saying. If you do ever get to Jersey

Glenn, on a quiet day
when all the poems are written and there's time,
well that might be — that *would* be — some day!

JOEY ON THE GARDEN PATH

Hello
Hello my name is Joe

Joe Stone
Joseph Stone

but people call me Hello Mrs Pray
it's a good day I mean I mean Good day

I wondered if
I was wondering if

your paper's been delivered
all right to the right standard

It has? I'm glad to hear that.
I'll be able to report that

to my seniors late today.
I was Hello Mr Pray

thank you all of you Prays and any other
children you do have for this clear answer

about my daily work
Goodbye and and good luck

CHIEF WARDEN MOUNTING A CUPBOARD

If I might just have quiet, thank you thank you
    another of my speeches, Mrs Kimble,
        turning a right old Winnie as you say!
If I might just if I might just have quiet,
    pipe down new arrivals someone help me.
        As some of you have rightly inferenced
the transport set for eighteen hundred hours
    did not arrive at eighteen hundred hours
        or for that matter nineteen hundred hours
or for that matter pipe down pipe down
    twenty hundred hours. It is technically
        now dark and the latest information
is as of now not in. No I don't agree
    there is no information. There is
        information. What there isn't yet
is latest information. I, like you, sir,
    am not in a situation of my personal
        choosing. I do therefore recommend
you do prepare yourselves to spend . . . Please!
    a second night please please!
        Nobody's listening.
I might as well be singing a nice song
    for all the bleedin *There'll be bluebirds over*
        the white cliffs of Dover . . . No one's noticed.
That's the latest information I have, sir,
    is it too late for your liking?

THE PRAY GIRLS AT THE BANDSTAND
IN THE SUMMER IN THE PARK

You—deliver our papers. You're Joe.
        I'm Sally. Mummy said you were a Jew
but Daddy said you weren't. You're half what?
        That might get pretty difficult for you,
what with this carry-on. Jule, his lot
        are teaming up with Hitler. No you are.
He brings the papers so he ought to know.
        Or maybe he doesn't read or he doesn't care,
it's bad news either way. So he doesn't mind
        delivering what he doesn't understand!
Maybe. That's a funny-looking bike.
        You can walk with us, we're going for ice cream.
You can buy them if you want. Or you could talk
        Italian. You can't oh that's a shame.
Perhaps if we lost the war we'd have to speak
        Italian or German when outside.
Our plan is—can I tell him? Suicide.

SALLY EATS A SUNDAE NEAR THE BANDSTAND IN THE PARK

Mummy says it's pointless going. It comes
    It comes, she says, they'll have us where they please,
City, country, Hitler's got gas bombs
    I read about it, think about it: *gas.*

Our road had a big practice, with a bell
    That means the gas is coming, you can't see it
You can only smell it. If you've no sense of smell
    Or you're elderly it's likely you're too late,

You're standing there but dead. Anyway the gas bell
    Was just like our school bell, I told them that,
I told them they should change that. The gas rattle,
    That's like a football rattle, Harry said,

It sounds like in the stands at West Ham.
    I really need to use a certain place.
Look at the queue. I'm an imbecile I am.
    It melted with me yakking on like this.

JOEY AND JULIE AT THE PICNIC TABLE

There she goes your sister Sally
sewing socks for soldiers try
saying that with a mouth full there's no way
there's nothing like an ice cream on a warm day
there's nothing like it
                    You're the paper boy.

I'm Joseph Stone.
                    Do you know
about this paste they make?
                    No, what paste?

You don't know anything. It's a new paste
they make my father said and it can mend
whatever's broken if you have things broken.
I have four things broken.

What were they?
                    They were mine.
My grenadiers.
                    Grenadiers? You mean,
like soldiers?
                    For a present round the tree.
They came in a presentation box. My father
wrapped it in gold paper
                              Oh at Christmas
at Christmas and he wrapped in the same paper
a book The Wonder Book of Do You Know
do you know it?

It's funny being asked
a question by a person who won't ever
look at you.
    I won't ever.

What's funny?
    I wasn't laughing. I meant funny
but I meant odd.

My father meant the Wonder Book for me.
He meant the soldiers for my brother Robert.
Things got muddled up. My older brother
said it made no sense a girl with soldiers.

It's unusual.
    Why don't you look away
if it's so very odd.

But you liked them, these soldiers.
And it isn't odd.
    I called them grenadiers.
My older brother
    Harry?
      said they're not
grenadiers at all and Robert said
he hated the stinking book of Do You Know.
Which made him change his mind, he did my father
on Boxing Day he stepped into our room
my sister and me and here you are he said
Julia's Regiment.

Robert had to read an hour a day
a chapter from the Wonder Book. As time went by
he said he's learning everything there is
and when he gets to the end of the Wonder Book
I better watch my back and then last week
I heard it shut.

Sally's ice cream's now an ice cream drink.
And a wasp home.

                Let me move it out of your way.

Are they gone.

            If . . . you looked at me I could tell you.
I can hear they're gone.

              I can hear the merry-go-round.

Paste, don't think I can help you there, Julie.
Do you mind if I call you Julia, or Julie?
I'm always seeing you up there at your window,
the bay window.

My window's at the back of where I live,
and all I see's the blessed railway.

They disappeared. When I found them
they were each spoiled. One was nut-coloured
and crooked from a fire
and another had the face scratched off. His face
was like the Tin Man's face have you seen that one?

There's a Tin Man, it was just like him, not real.
Blank but with a uniform, this paste
someone could use to paste the colour on,
the skin colour.
                    One was painted pink.
So a girl would want it it was painted pink.

And my favourite one who I told my sister Sally
I liked because I liked his face I called him
the princely one. Well Sally only told him.
The one who did it all and the princely one
Your brother did all this?
                    Now he has no head.

Paste could help with that. Do you have the head?

If you had, had it, it could.

Pink paint would wash off, wouldn't it. It would.
If they're melted, I don't know . . .
                    It's a new paste.
You don't know a thing about it.
Do you spend time do you Joe in factories?
You can call me Joe.
                    Will you look for it for me?

Something to mend my soldiers?
                    Yes I will.
Yes. I'll always look, until I find it.

But you're looking at me right now.
How do you know?

Because when Robert was out
I took the Wonder Book of Do You Know
from off his shelf so I know everything.
You know everything. You know the wonders.
I do, I know the wonders.
And that's why
you stare out of the window. All the wonders
are out there somewhere!
That's exactly why.
I stare if it's still enough, which is very late
or early. I pretend that it goes still
for me.
But I see you early.
Come late.
At midnight but you have to be as still
as everything is.
Why?
Because the earth
changes at that time. And things you know
aren't true.
I don't know much!
But still the earth
has got you on its back and it does know
where you're going.
It shouldn't be out in the blackout!

Should it, in the blackout.
What blackout?

Will you let me look at the men, at the grenadiers?
Perhaps they can all be mended.

They're here.

I beg your pardon?

You're looking at them now.

That's your right hand, Julie.

Grenadiers.

I told you there were four. You think they're fingers
but you said you don't know much and they all heard you.
Until somebody mends them they'll be here.
The leader and the ranger,
the silent one and the princely one,
they all survived. What thing was done to them
was all in vain. Look at them come together.

Now they part, to take on the world.
Good luck they say.

There are five though.

The thumb, was he a soldier?

You should know.

He's you. Look my sister.

HARRY IN THE DARK

Can't sleep. I can't remember
    How to sleep.
I made an enormous effort
    I was counting sheep

On a green Snowdonian hillside,
    Only I saw
About a hundred farmers counting
    Thousands more.

So I started counting fish.
    I too had gills.
I was growing faster than I swam
    And something else

Was starting to count me.
    It's only nine.
Move your blasted elbow Robby
    This bit's mine.

Let's everyone tell a story,
    At least a joke?
I know I know I know I can hear
    We're firing back

It's us it's us I know that sound
    No worries Mum.
We're blowing Hans and Gunter back
    To kingdom come.

The life-strength of the British, that's
    A phrase you might
Remember from the PM
    It's all right all right

All right, the city's black as coal
    They're flying blind.
It's probably clouding over too,
    I shouldn't mind

A little rain tomorrow, no?
    Some light relief.
I've had enough of summertime
    For one life.

The summertime's with them, the sun's
    A brazen spy.
The moon's with them, a bright eye
    Or a dark eye.

All those afternoons of cricket
    All those nights
At camp they were just watching us
    For bloody Fritz.

It's too good to be true, sometimes I
    Had that sense
When the sun was breaking through. In fact
    I said so once.

Thought it went quite quiet, thought
    The sun went still.
All our shadows waiting
    On its signal.

Our allies are the clouds and rain
    Our mercy fleet
Out over the Atlantic
    And no sign of it.

ROBBY LIGHTING A CANDLE WHICH HE BLOWS OUT AT THE END

Rotted from within
then smitten from without.
Harry's not the only Churchill here.
Rotted from within
then smitten from without.

What's that about, Jew-seppy, any clues?
You been rotten lately,
been smitten? Got any life-strength? I can tell you
get me some ice cream now and I will personally
be your blimmin slave for the duration.

Imagine that, slaving for Jew-seppy.
Mixing the four flavours. More sugar,
Master, more ice?
Gelato, chocolato. That's the future,
I'm telling you, there'll always be an England,

except no English in it. *I say, Führer,*
a shade more schockolade if you please,
and a cherry girl on top.
We'll live in our gingerbread mansion, won't we Joey,
on hundreds and bloody thousands.

Been smitten, Dennis Medland?
He's sitting up,
I can see him no I won't leave him alone.
I want to know what he did with Albie Rogers.
He swallowed him. I hated Albie Rogers

he hated me
but it's no excuse to eat him, is it Dennis?
We still doing speeches, Harry?
Did I mention *there is a malignancy in our midst*?
I already did? Fair do's.

All right there, Dennis? *Rotted from within.*
Smitten from without. I'm only quoting,
only quoting Churchill like *mine brooder.*
Once upon a time . . .
this was Harry's idea, the flaming stories.

Once upon a time
there was a gent called Albie but *unfortunately*
he died. Ever play that game?
Mum, you remember our storytelling game?
Mum's asleep. Good job.

So *unfortunately* he died.
Fortunately he survived in a new form
as the man who mislaid his daughter.
Unfortunately he hid in the same pisshole
as Mr Robert Pray who *fortunately*

married Miss Greer Garson.
Unfortunately for Dennis I got eyesight.
Fortunately for Dennis it's pitch black.
Unfortunately for Joey he's an eye-tie.
Fortunately for Joey . . . oh dear THE END.

RAUL FIXING A COSMOPOLITAN

See old Joey's sat back in his window.
I'm telling you in all of New York City
how many joints is that? Just yesterday,
Clint, you walk in here. You got the world
to choose from, and you didn't want nobody
taking all your time! Now it's tomorrow

and you look like shit. Stay at home tomorrow,
see your family, sit in your own window.
I'm kidding, hey. Don't like nobody
can't take my kidding. It's the New York City
style, you know it is, you seen the world
you like it here. It's another awesome day.

It's another peach it's just like yesterday.
I was kidding with you. Come back tomorrow,
Clint, the old guy will. Where else in the world
is he expected? Ain't no other window
waiting for the guy, no other city
left to move to. I never heard nobody

want to move from this. I mean nobody
left alone. Man I can't take Sunday.
It's slow, it crawls, Sunday in this city.
Hello? Yeah this is him. Not tomorrow?
Lemme write that down. Sun in the freakin window
blinding me. I got it. Stop the world

for breaking news . . . *What? Yeah 'on the world'*
I know, I got it. Ciao. Okay. Nobody
gets to know. Hey, Joe, what's in the window?
See some babes? Can't be your lucky day
it's mine. Clint says he's stopping by tomorrow.
He wants to hear you bombed that Nazi city

back to the stone age. I said 'Nazi city'
Joey, I was kidding. What in the world
do I care, kill a Nazi guy tomorrow,
lighten up. I haven't told nobody,
Clint, remember I told you this — that day
was it yesterday when Joey was in his window?

That there ain't nobody else in New York City
paid so high? Windows on the World.
Tuesday I start. Tomorrow's my last day.

III

Once upon a time there was a princess. But she didn't live in a castle she lived in a boatyard. She lived in a boatyard and she looked around for princes or kings or queens to talk to, but all she ever saw was boats.

Do you mind me telling you this? Because you know, I'm going to anyway.

One day the princess whose name was Princess Alice admitted she herself was in fact a boat. She hadn't understood, she wasn't Alice or even Princess Alice she was *The Princess Alice*. And by the time she'd taken all of that in, someone had bust a bottle of champagne over her arse and she was sliding down the gangway into the Thames.

How do I know this? Well I'll tell you. I was the captain of *The Princess Alice*. Yes, the captain was Captain Medland and he said: 'Alice, you're not a warship or a battleship and you're not an ocean liner. You're a paddle steamer, girl. And you and I are going to sail east and west and up the river and down for the marvellous folk of the East End of London. And we're going to have such fun.'

And that's exactly what they did for many years. But unfortunately, to quote another storyteller, nothing lasts forever. One beautiful afternoon, in the year of eighteen hundred and seventy-eight, so late in the summer it's autumn, so early in autumn it's summer, she sailed out to

Sheerness in a festive mood, did Alice, and the six hundred marvellous folk of the East End of London sailed with her in their Sunday best, their hats, their parasols. And they picnicked on the banks of the Thames and strolled this way and that. And then they picked up all their picnic things and sailed on *The Princess Alice* in an home-sweet-home direction.

What a beautiful evening it was. The sound of the paddle, the silvery splash of laughter and the ripple of conversation, and the squeals of the marvellous children of the East End of London.

And they came to Gallions Reach, and they passed by Gallions Reach, and as Alice rounded the riverbank in the coppery evening light, what do you think she saw?

She saw a most fantastical sight, a sight she had always dreamed of, since the time she was young and still believed she was a princess with a crown, and not a pleasure-boat with a paddle.

She saw a castle rising from the river, and she cried out to Captain Medland: 'Oh, you don't know how long I've been searching for that castle!'

But it wasn't just any castle. It was *The Bywell Castle* and not a single passenger or picnicker on Alice had the ghost of an idea that it was too late. Too late in the day to get past *The Bywell Castle*. Not even with a *by your leave*. Not even with an *excuse me*.

It came nearer and nearer, and its pilot danced to one side, and Captain Medland knew the dance and danced off to the other side, but they might as well have been waltzing in air for all the good it did now.

For there was still the sound of the paddle, and the silvery splash of laughter, and the ripple of conversation, and the squeals of the marvellous children of the East End of London. That all continued for a while. But then it grew quieter and quieter and quieter, until all you could hear was the sound of the paddle and the cry of the little princess: 'My castle! My castle!'

And *The Bywell Castle* stared and grew enormous and they met.

And my poor princess was sliced in half and we went into the water.

But it wasn't really water, it was everything the marvellous wealthy people up West had vomited in the toilet. It was sewage and we spluttered in it, and those who hadn't drowned already drowned in it and I quote:

> *Half a boat to port,*
> *Half a boat to starboard.*
> *Into the valley of shit*
> *Floated the six hundred.*

My name is Captain Dennis Medland. I am ninety-nine years old and I am also Poet Laureate.

And strange as it seems, I saved them.

I saved everybody. And I laid them on the bank in rows all shivering and stinking. And when there were none left, and nothing floating on the water, I took the deepest breath in the world and dived into the filthy Thames and swam through the black horror, downwards, downwards, to where my little princess lay broken on the riverbed.

And I lifted the two pieces. And I put them back together. And she smiled because she knew me. And I brought her back to the surface and I washed the filth away.

Then I baptised her Mary.

That's my story.

JOEY LEANING FORWARD

What's in the yellow envelope? Oh it's nothing,
it's nothing,

you don't want to be bothered by it,
I bring it with me sometimes, it's

nothing,
it's just something

committed to paper, you know,
my element, the paper boy. You too. But God knows

you've heard enough from me.
That's kind of you to say.

But there's not much else to tell.
The bombs fell.

People told jokes and stories. People sang
There'll Always Be an England. I saw my gran,

in the room across from me, I swear I never
saw her so happy, Glenn. They liked to stick together,

the old ones. Then I think at around eleven
maybe ten, maybe eleven,

the mum woke up and the baby woke up
and the stories stopped

and they had a right old barney,
the Prays, they'd have said a *barney*,

an argument, a row,
about some heirlooms — *Where the hell are they now?*

the mother went on shrieking. One of the sons
had thought the other son

had dug them from the flowerbed
where the mum said they were buried.

Nobody took the blame.
She was very distressed, the mum,

there were tantrums and tears.
'Mum.' I have not said that word in forty years.

And I may well require a scotch in the near future.
It is not — it was not my nature

to do what I did then.
But in all the atrocious din,

the ack-ack, the sirens, the mines, the bombs,
the children shouting the mums

hysterical I started to hear music.
Some sort of — march time — music,

a tune with no ending.
And I found myself—I was standing

and the brothers saw I was because with the light
flashing and flickering I was a silhouette.

And they asked in their own ways what exactly I thought
I was playing at.

And I asked in a voice where exactly
the things were buried, and the mother simply told me.

And I went. I was getting the hell out of that place.
A scotch Raul and whatever the hell he has.

Nobody tried to stop me. Truth be told
they were laughing, people were laughing. And an old

gentleman said could you please find my garden
and mow the lawn while you're at it, and the warden's

murmuring what in heaven's name does it matter . . .
But I remember feeling better,

except I've tried my damnedest to avoid
that bog room all this time and of course I need it.

I stop there in the dark,
do my stuff and I'm a mess, I'm a wreck

as I know I can't go back,
I can still hear laughing. I know if I go back

I'm the wop forever, the little yellow wop.
Kids, you know, that crap.

I clean myself and I'm shaking but I'm strong.
Right or wrong it's done now, it's done,

I'll get to Hermit Road and I'll return
with all their beloved things. I turn

and I'm striding for the door,
when I hit my head and I'm cursing and it's her.

I don't recall any pain, I recall the smell
of the dark I left behind, that smell

's an ever-present
flavour to that moment . . .

And it must have hurt,
but still she doesn't say a single word

she lifts her hand and holds it to her brow
a moment there. By now

the school had quietened down. They must have thought
I'd gone. And they hadn't noticed yet

the girl had crept away.
I see her by the window and the sky

is smashed with light behind her so her hair
is lit with it, then it's dark and she's still there,

Julie,
I wanted to say, I wanted to say *Julie.*

What I said instead
was I couldn't take her with me. It wasn't hard

to say it, it was true,
I couldn't take her I said I can't take you

too dangerous! But I'd be an hour at the most
I said I'm a London boy I won't get lost,

and all your family's here.
To all of this she stood there

mute and dark, with her little hands by her sides,
with the pounding worse than ever. And I realised

she wasn't going to move unless I did
what I had to do, John Wayne, what I now did,

I moved to her,
I took a step towards her

expecting that like all the girls I knew
she'd shy away she'd have to

so I took a step but she didn't move and the heat
from her face, from the dirt and sweat

I was breathing and her eyes were two holes
black glittering black jewels

and you know I thought I'll hold her in the blackout
all my life but she shivered as we met,

Glenn, she did shy away and I move again
she moves again

and I spread my arms as if to hold her fast
but I mean to herd her backwards like a lost

animal to her kind.
At the door of classroom seven she turns round

and her brother calls her name and I just run.
Now I was the lost one.

As I went out I saw a clock at midnight,
but I witnessed daylight, or a frozen daylight,

an afternoon,
or stepping from a film into an afternoon

I ran across the playground—
the *playground*—

we'd been watching like bad children
thirty hours. For nothing. In the heavens

hell, the onslaught. I had to tilt my mind
to take it in. Wind tunnels and the wind

a smoke that gripped me by the lungs
and bullied me along

I was running north—where the family lived was north—
to the south there was no south

there was no sky
there was no sky to see

just chaos over us all,
there was just there was just this chaos over us all.

Billowing worlds of black,
the city this dire red. I turned my back

on everything and ran,
I knew the roads I ran on,

I was the paper boy,
I'm still the paper boy,

running from memory,
moving between the fires that suddenly

ignited by themselves, though there were streets
that wouldn't catch a thing, deserted streets

all fogged and dead I ran down, and known streets
now long blue ghastly sites

of monuments and holes. I found
a bike in one of those and I'd understand

if someone needed mine, I called out as I rode,
and I got to Hermit Road

in about an hour, I think, after one o'clock.
I'd heard a clock

chime if it was true. And when I reached
the rubble of their house I began to search.

The worst was done
on Hermit Road. The people had all gone.

Nobody came or went, nobody passed.
There were soft explosions off to the southwest

but it was dark and quiet for a time.
I knelt down, I've done this in a dream.

And for a while I even heard my breath.
I laid my hands on the soil of the cool earth.

Then I dug where the mother had said.
I dug where the brothers had said,

I dug up every piece of earth still there
and found no box, no heirlooms, no treasure.

I heard a sound, a footstep, quite near,
I hid in the ruins. Finally I'm here

I thought, in the family parlour, well that's nice.
What a lovely place

you have. Honey, Joey? Or marmalade?
Thank you very much indeed, homemade.

Ruins. I could hear
a man was talking but I wasn't sure

if anyone was with him. I *was* sure
I had to get back to the school, it would take an hour

when I did see something gleaming there, a book.
I knelt and found a glossy blue-black

company ledger it was.
TATE AND LYLE it said in a gold gloss.

I shook the plaster off it
and dirt and opened it

and I leafed through a million numbers till they stopped
suddenly, as if they'd added up

to nothing, pages of nothing.
Then there was all this writing.

But the blessed railway is only reconised by Joseph Stone the paper boy. The blessed railway only appears in the morning; it only appears a minute before first thing in the morning. So I made myself wake up then at that time. For example it was morning but not first thing in the morning. I wrote OUR NAMES in the water my breath made on the window pane; then I went downstares on tiptoe and every single stare creaked; I tiptoed past the parlour and I saw the wireless sitting there.

I HAVE SAID ALL I WANT TO SAY, it said, THERE IS NO MORE.

I carefully turned the key in the door and opened the door to the very cold world;

All that was there was the same as ever. Everything was frozen to death. There were no lights on so no one in the whole entire universe knew we were there because if they would do, they would form into formations;

It goes from far away to near and it goes from near to far away. It is the blessed railway line that has appeard in our street this morning. I see my face in the trembling rails and ANOTHER FACE. Joey is not here with me as I stand at the blessed railway line; but his face is on the trembling rails and I look at him for quite a time but while I do NO TIME PASSES;

Do   you   know   the   sugar   place;
"   "   "   "   sugar   place;
~~Lantern~~ lights   "   sugar   place;
Master

Do   you   know   the   wonder   books;
"   "   "   "   "   "
~~Sider~~ finds
~~Slider Sider Slider~~
~~Crosser~~
~~Crowsfoot~~
~~Cruler~~   ~~Crewler~~   ~~Chur~~

Lodger says   ~~Clue~~   ~~Coil~~
THERE IS   ~~Curl~~
A   ~~Wicked~~
MALIGNACY   ~~Wick~~   ~~Coyl~~
IN OUR MIDST;   ~~Slick~~
                       ~~Sly~~ says

Rhyme:
"O London won't be London long"
"for it will all be pulled down"
"and I will sing a funerel song"

~~Stone says there is nothing like an ice cream on a~~
~~warm day;~~

"Soon we shall be there I hope" said he.

Julieta did not have to hope they would be; she knew the train was ONE MILE ONLY from the gates of the Crystal County;

She looked out of the window at the lavander fields going by; and she looked into the eyes of him and saw the same fields; amazingly;

She looked back afar at the aweful twisting smoke; of the dark damp city and she observed that the whole place had got up into a tower and it was standing on the horison with its long wire like arms held out. WHAT IS WRONG JULIETA?

She turned her back on the question and said to her princely one "We shall be there presently"

MAN OUT OF THE BLUE

Live here do you? I live here. London I mean. Got a book?

That's good. Got a bedside light? Only joking. Got the lights, ain't yer, son, got the Christmas lights. Whee. Bang. And the Christmas crackers.

Going to the dogs on Friday? I am. I always do go.

I live here. Londoner. Match on Saturday. You going? Go on you Irons. Bang, one-nothin. Foreman.

Bit of a reader myself. Might go down I dunno to the library for a read. Might do when I'm done.

Done for the day I might. I better be going.

Been good talking, though. You and me, son, readers.

On the first night of peace the only noise is secret and I
curtsey through the air;

I see him far below, the fields in squares diamonds and
~~parralelagrams~~ parallelagrams all round him he sleeps so
deeply;

The moon is whole and for the first time I remember it
doesn't matter the light;

When I have reached him there is no room left for him to
move; unless I feel it; it is the first night of peace;

The origenal still place of the Crystal Destination looks the
way it always will;

I try to find my list I made of goodbyes to say; but what I
find eventuelly is not in my writing;

'Goodbye' is what he hears me say when he wakes up
inside; his mouth opens O but all I'm in the middle of
saying is 'Goodbye means God be with you'! I'm with you
too I say! Goodbye I'm with you Joey!

We part away again because in this relm we live in it all
begins again and over breakfast we know nothing; we
intruduce ourselves; the little strip between the gold
curtains is blue; so it is either the blue of a frozen morning
or the blue of a ~~beuatiful~~ beautiful day; he says shall we go
and look but I do not know him yet; that will begin; I turn

I shut the book.
My pal was back.

I ran to the bike and pedalled off
but my chain broke. He's saying the same old stuff

You fancy us for the Cup, son?
So I ditch the bike and break into a run

and he runs alongside panting till he's done,
then I hear him say *Can't do it, you go on*

and he falls behind. The fires are up ahead
and I'm pounding down this wide deserted

street when I stop to think.
I didn't find their treasures. I found one thing,

and I must bring it back,
it's Julie's book I said aloud *your book,*

this is the way my mind was going—it's gone,
I was never supposed to see it, the Joey Stone

inside was never meant to, to see it.
So I'd never see it again but I want to see it.

I mean to have it by me
somehow, always, by me.

Though it felt wrong
it feels wrong —

it's a voice
it was like the only voice

to have spoken of me, ever.
It simply felt — it seemed — time spent together.

So I find on this same street a broken door
and a front room where the glow of all the fire

is just about enough to read it by.
I'm a ghost among the things of a family

so I find an excellent pencil in a drawer
and letter-writing paper and I squat there

in some bits of a family home,
scribbling on their paper, with the name

J. G. FAIRFIELD heading every sheet.
I start to copy it out,

neatly as I can in the filth and the heat,
listening for footsteps, dropping out of sight

as a fireman hurries by then some Home Guard.
Planes right overhead,

bombers, suddenly thumps
that shake the floor. Some bombs

come close enough to bring their pictures down,
the Fairfield family and I'm writing on

methodically, not once rereading,
not *reading*,

just copying what's there. And while I write
I'm thinking of the Prays, wondering why I'm late

He should be back by now,
Harry's saying. Should be dead by now,

says Robby, old Jew-seppy, what a shame,
he's laughing, what are we going to do for ice cream?

And Sally would be sad,
she'd cry a bit and then she'd say I'd died

a hero, helping others, us . . . And *she?*
Now she'd speak, to the joy of the family

now she'd speak and they'd know it was more than Joe
the paper boy, now they'd know.

Good would come of it,
I was nodding that as I wrote,

and I wrote for a good two hours
a good two hours

I did this, this thing
you do, sir. Nothing hanging

on whether I do or not in the eyes of the world.
Whether I copy the daydreams of a girl

in secret or actually go back where she is.
Actually go back where she is,

actually burrow my way back to her side,
take up her hand like I'd

always do.
No. No no. I did the thing you do.

I wrote—you and me, writers—
I wrote till I reached the end and the Fairfield Papers,

as I called them, I hid away,
in my jacket, for some other day, today

who gives a damn and I shut the book.
This book

I'm afraid is all I found.
Nothing was where you said it was in the ground,

Mrs Pray,
it all got burned to a crisp or taken away

But they wouldn't mind
what I'd found or hadn't found

because I'd be alive, back from the dead!
You made it, Joey, good God!

cries Harry and once again
my brain just making it up. The Stone brain

coining it out of nothing. Off I go,
into the fire and the night again goes Joe

for nothing.
Just running.

Pour me another shot. Pour me another generous shot
of what you got.

Black Saturday,
Black Sunday,

Black Monday,
Black Tuesday,

the paper boy
goes by.

Be out of the picture soon.
Then you can carry on,

flatten the page, breathe in,
ah, dip the special pen,

nail the minute down.
Nail it to a cloud, call it your own

when it all's gone by.
I stagger round a corner and I see

suddenly there are three
not one not two but *three*

the ones they were waiting for a mile away,
three London buses painted grey

but gleaming orange with the flames and parked,
going nowhere. I run and climb in the back

of the last bus of the three,
and I ask the driver by any chance are they

heading for Canning Town?
Oh very funny, he says and he says *Step down*

this is a holiday service. And he looks mad,
so I do what he says and I mean he looks *British* mad

not angry he looks insane.
I run to the second bus and a beauty queen

is sitting in it, this blond hair cascading
out from her cap. I'm just about deciding

lies might get me somewhere, so I say:
Miss, I am alone, my family

are dead —
I sniffed — I am an orphan, I need a ride

to Canning Town to find my only last
relative, my grandma. And I'm lost!

She looks at her fingernails and says *I'm sorry
for all your troubles. But you got to talk to Terry.*

And she nods to the bus in front.
To Terry I say my parents died, my aunt

was blown to smithereens, I was shot, I was left for dead
I was tortured, and he's shaking his bald head

and saying *That's as may be, rules are rules*
when I suddenly think of saying There's something else,

mister. I know the way.
To Canning Town? Why dincha bloody say?

He turns the key and we start.
Behind us there's Mae West at the wheel, she starts

and she's giving me thumbs-up. When we take a bend
I see the last of the buses and their friend

just staring out of the glass.
And then I turn eyes front to witness a vast

explosion, and this rising stream
of light I'm lifted backwards through a long room

I notice as I go is an omnibus.
And when I'm not unconscious

I'm sitting in a place
I've a window seat and there's some broken glass

everywhere I think my ears are bleeding
but I hear my voice repeating and repeating

directions to the driver Agate Street
is the next street, the next street

is Agate Street the next street the next street.
But the driver's torn apart and there's no next street

for all there is is a castle wall of fire
and howling there

a frame
and a fireman like a stickman taking aim

his white
jet

turned to steam
in no time

TERRY LIFTED UP

In black and white it is and I can prove it.
Talk to the depot CAMDEN TOWN they told me
                    they told me

CAMDEN TOWN not CANNING TOWN I ask you
what am I to do I can only go
                  I can only go

by my directions wasn't till about
ooooooooooh . . . I dunno, five this afternoon?
                  late afternoon

round five o'clock I'm hearing CANNING TOWN
not CAMDEN TOWN I'm hearing CANNING TOWN.
                  CANNING TOWN?

the George that's right the George that's right he goes
rendezvous at the George for Hallsville School
                  Hallsville School

in CAMDEN TOWN no CANNING TOWN so what
George you mean he means the George at WANSTEAD
                  at WANSTEAD

you want me to go to WANSTEAD or CANNING TOWN
cos I can to WANSTEAD or CANNING TOWN
                  or CAMDEN TOWN

or PLUMSTEAD or BECKTON BOW
    BATTERSEA BRIGHTON BLACKPOOL

SHIFT CHANGE

Can I help you?
Can I help you?
    Sir, you're good to go, you've paid, you're cool.

You're waiting?
Oh you're waiting
    for someone in your party. Mr Stone?

In the bathroom?
No the bathroom's
    empty, Mr Stone, you mean the old guy

no he went home.
He went home
    oh I'd say twenty minutes back? What's that?

His envelope?
This envelope's
    not his, that's not his name, it's someone else's.

Where? Right here.
Written right here.
    For Glenn, Poet and Gentleman. This you?

Yes and no?
Yes and no?
    Yes you're a poet or yes you're a gentleman? Sir?

THE SUGAR MILE

for Joseph Stone

I wrote at the top of breath
not having reached it. At the top of breath

the skyline is a shoreline
seen from high above. Buildings are sand

and peter out. All land
is a ledge, all space is a drop, all steps have a nerve.

There can be no first person.
I fill my lungs to go and the first person's

yards ahead. Then he jumps.
Then I look and he falls and falls until my lungs

are veal and I'm alone.
I write *I* and it leaks like a first inkpen.

The poet is any stranger
seen today, whose past is an empty notebook

~~tugged from a pocket, laid~~
~~sealed on the bar like this one is. He shifts~~

~~and it's evening in a mirror~~
~~peek a boo through a platoon of optics~~

whose past is an empty moleskine

~~tugged from the ruins of~~

~~whose past is an empty moleskine~~